# Contents

GW01071925

# Foreword

Are you starting the great game of camping? Rest assured that you will find fun and adventure in doing new things, travelling to new scenes, and discovering for yourself a way of life that gives opportunity for enjoying more fresh air than all the other sports and pastimes put together.

With 'bed in the bush and stars to see' you can find quiet and companionship—time to listen to the voice of the wild. Leave behind the noise and sham of city life and find how little man needs to be content.

You will gain health and self-reliance, and find that the greatest pleasures lie in simple things. Camping will help you to pit your strength against the might of mountains and the surge of great rivers down to the sea.

*G. A. Leubitt.*

Director General
The Camping and Caravanning Club

# The tent

'Camping' is something of a generic term and in most countries means camping with any type of mobile equipment. For the purposes of this book we are interpreting the term as meaning camping with a tent.

It follows, therefore, that you cannot even start camping until you have acquired a tent, as this forms the basic form of shelter around which all the ancillary equipment is centred. Tents come in a variety of shapes and sizes and, although designs have changed over the years, they can be categorised into definite groups according to their intended use.

## The single pole tent

The simplest form of tent is probably the sort which is supported at the centre by a single pole and around which is draped the canvas in the form of a cone (the 1914–18 army type 'bell tent' is a typical example based on this rudimentary form). If the base is then secured with ties to the ground, it presents an extremely firm structure, capable of standing up to very high winds, whilst being very effective at throwing off any water which may strike it in the form of rain (see Fig. 1a and 1b).

Derivations of this simple design can be seen in the Black's Itisa and Good Companion series of tents. They are quick to erect and have more than stood the test of time in both their popularity and excellence of service. Normally they are square in shape rather than rounded and can take up to two campers who are able to sit up when inside. They usually have an inner section with a sewn-in ground-sheet and an outer flysheet which is pegged out directly to the ground. The most common materials used are cotton for the inner section and siliconised nylon for the outer flysheet.

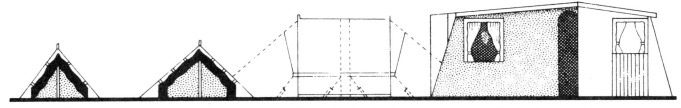

*Fig. 1a 'Pup' or 'A' tent (single pole)*

*Fig. 1b Wall tent (single pole)*

*Fig. 2a 'Cottage' tent*

*Fig. 2b Frame tent*

# The ridge tent

This type of tent somewhat resembles the pitched roof of a house and in its simplest form is square-ended. It is sometimes called a 'cottage tent' for that reason, too. The ridge itself on larger models is actually a horizontal pole, supported at each end by a vertical pole directly onto the ground. Without the canvas there is no stability at all, but once pegged out and with suitable guy ropes at each end, it becomes both rigid and roomy and will sleep any number of people according to its overall size (see Fig. 3).

*Fig. 3 Standard ridge tent*

On the smaller versions, which can sleep only one or at most two people, the ridge pole is not always included. Instead, the part of the fabric which would normally cover it at the ridge position is reinforced. When pegged out, the smaller size of such a tent scarcely allows any noticeable sag at the top as the end guy rope pulls it taut. This enables the 'ironmongery' (the poles) to be kept to an absolute minimum and so helps economise on weight. Such a tent, therefore, is popular among those who are weight conscious in their approach to camping.

A variation on the frame or poles of this type of tent is to use an 'A' pole construction instead of a single pole at one or sometimes both ends. Although this is counter-productive in weight saving, it has the very definite advantage that the inverted 'V' so formed gives free passage both to the entrance and to the rear bell-end which is now almost standard on these 'pup' tents as they have become known.

For such tents designed specifically for use under wet and arduous weather conditions, 'A' frame designs are used externally, so that the tent is hung from them. This avoids getting the interior wet during erection as a sewn-in groundsheet is invariably in the design. Such tents normally have a separate, loose flysheet which is afterwards draped over the tops of the poles and then pegged out via short guy ropes at intervals along its periphery (see Fig 4). This forms a convenient space between the two layers of canvas, so that the inner section is kept dry if a minimal amount of spray happens to settle on it. In that way packing up becomes easier, since the inner tent is virtually bone dry other than for the underside of the groundsheet, which can, of course, be wiped dry before folding.

A further modification sometimes found on specialist tents such as these is a large horizontal valance at the base, on which can be heaped rocks or stones to secure the tent when the nature of the ground makes it impossible to use pegs. If all else fails, fore and aft guy ropes may then be secured by

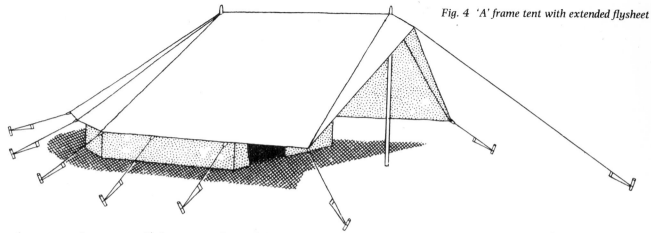

*Fig. 4 'A' frame tent with extended flysheet*

pitons (rope securing pegs which are hammered into rocks by climbers). This type of tent is mainly designed for use in mountain country.

One other use of the ridge tent is for small group camping—as with a family—but here, the design is much larger and rather more involved. Normally three 'A' pole sections are used, plus two ridge poles which join them together. This forms the area of the sleeping and the living sections. The canvas then provides a hemi-spherical 'bell-end' at each extremity, giving plenty of floor space but not too much head room except at the centre, which is normally about six feet high internally.

At one end, a bedroom or bedrooms are hung, each with its sewn-in groundsheet. Both sloping sections of the living area may together or separately be raised to a horizontal position to be supported by guy ropes and full length poles, forming an awning. It gives the choice of total or partial opening, with increased headroom, according to the direction of wind; or one or both may be kept closed when rainy.

This style of large, family tent—although, as already mentioned, not over roomy in terms of headroom—does provide a superbly reliable shelter if the weather decides to blow really hard. Many families who camp regularly under all conditions favour them to some of the more recent and 'luxurious' tents.

# The frame tent

The 'frame tent', as it has become known, refers to the large chalet-like tent which descended on the U.K. market in the early fifties. It was a French invention, based perhaps on the sort used by wandering tribesmen in the Sahara Desert—except that the latter used goat skins. At the end of the Second World War families started looking around for a convenient holiday form within the average person's pocket. Thus the frame tent was born and for many years enjoyed an unprecedented explosion in sales throughout much of the world. Its particular appeal probably lay in the design which allowed for separate bedroom compartments, zipped up to keep out insects, and which gave a large living space with full headroom (see Fig. 5).

So, cooking units on stands, tables and chairs, etc, became the order of the day. To the Continental camper especially, who tended to put his tent on site for the whole season, it became—and still is—the vogue among family campers, a position to be usurped perhaps only by the growing popularity of the trailer tent (see page 9).

## Other tents

One other type or category of small tent includes the 'dome' and the 'tunnel'. Both are what they seem. The first is shaped in dome formation and the second as a similar diameter tunnel with sloping ends. Frame support is normally by small diameter aluminium alloy tubes which separate into short lengths for easy transportation. They are very much into the specialist climber market and are extremely light in weight. Survival rather than comfort is the prime consideration and both are extremely cramped for space. An alternative to aluminium tubing is fibreglass rod, which is sometimes seen in use with such designs.

*Fig. 5  Frame tents*

# The construction of tents

## The flysheet

Tents vary enormously in their design and materials but the common factor lies in their almost universal two-part construction: a fundamental tent and a flysheet in some shape or form. We see it in the basic single pole and ridge tents and it is also repeated in the frame tent—except that the detail is not the same. So a 'tent' can be the main shelter, protected further by a separate flysheet; or it can be a much lighter, more flimsy affair, around which is placed the 'outer tent' that goes right down to the ground and provides the shelter. In such cases, what we in effect have is a modified flysheet. (A flysheet is always necessary when using cotton as a fabric, since it relies on plenty of aeration to keep it impermeable.)

If the tent is touched whilst wet, then the water will be primed into the fabric and will temporarily destroy its waterproof properties; if the inner section can be kept virtually dry, this will not happen. It is important, therefore, not to touch the inside of the living area in a frame tent. A number of manufacturers actually provide a head liner in white cotton material, which also adds to the overall brightness by acting as a reflector—especially at night.

## Material

Years ago, only one type of material was acceptable—cotton canvas, in varying weights according to the size of the tent. Then, as requirements from increasing lightweight markets were for lighter and lighter specifications to suit backpackers and mountaineers, so the use of specially siliconised nylon fabrics was adopted. Ingenious weaves incorporating fishnet type 'rip stop' features were added, so that the smallest tent need weigh no more than $2\frac{1}{2}$ to 3 lbs.

This material is still not strong enough, of course, for the bigger tent, and cotton continues to dictate the scene. However, some advances have been made with man-made fibres in Dacron-acrylic, which, because it is dyed in the thread before weaving, does not fade over many years of use. PVC coating of some fabrics enables these to be used on frame tent roofs, since a build-up of rainwater frequently encountered at that point tends to encourage leaks in the living area.

## Tent poles

Tent poles were always made in timber at one time. Now, the use of either aluminium alloy or lightweight steel tubing, zinc coated to keep off rust, is generally accepted, except in the case of very big semi-marquee style tents.

## Pegs

Pegs, too, have undergone considerable change. All tent pegs used to be made of wood and were very bulky as a result. Nowadays a whole array of different types in zinc plated steel are available to the modern camper. Even grades of nylon are not uncommon, but they tend to break up if the ground is at all hard—and in any case will not take extensive hammering.

Which type you use will depend on the sort of camping you do, the size of the tent, and to some degree the terrain on which you are pitching. Weather, too, may determine whether you need to add extra storm guys to combat gale-force winds. Small tents erected on soft turf can usually get away with 'skewer' type pegs which can normally be pushed in by hand. 'Samson' type steel pegs are fairly universal in their application, whilst in very sandy soil even the old-fashioned wooden pegs—quite large ones in fact—should be used at least at every corner position. In very dry ground, as is met in Southern France. Spain, Italy or Greece, only the best of the steel variety stand a chance. Even then it is advisable to carry several spares.

There are special pullers, too, for extracting tent pegs, usually with a horizontal wooden handle and a steel hook which will pull out the pegs quite easily.

# Guy ropes

Other than on very large tents, guy ropes made from nylon are now widely used. They do not rot and can also be manufactured in bright colours so that people are less prone to trip over them on site. They do not stretch and, of course, with this factor comes another advantage inasmuch as they do not shrink. This means they have less tendency to pull out their pegs at inopportune moments, such as in the middle of a rainy night or when you are not around to make the necessary adjustment to the tension. Most tents these days incorporate rubber tensioners at the base of the side walls, or sometimes at the ends of their guy ropes. These will take the buffeting of winds and relieve the strain on the pegs. There are special storm guys for extremely bad weather conditions, which normally secure the strategic corner positions on frame tents or the tops of the poles in other designs. Storm poles too are available. These are placed internally, fixed diagonally across any panels which need reinforcing.

# Choosing a tent

When making a choice, the first considerations lie with your personal requirements, governed also by the amount of camping you intend to do and where or when you intend to do it. If you are a single person looking for a convenient means of cheap overnight accommodation only and are intending to restrict your activities to the summer season, then a fairly simple 'pup' ridge tent should suit you. Subsequent considerations are how you will carry it. If it is to be on your back, then much thought must be given to the overall weight factor. A backpacker ought not to exceed 25 lb to 30 lb total weight, including his rucksack, or he will certainly begin to regret it as he walks. So a tent which will not exceed 3–4 lbs should be sought. (It is surprising just how much the weight can be controlled if you shop around.)

If you intend to use the tent as shelter when pursuing a fairly strenuous sport throughout the year, such as mountaineering in one form or another, then only the best of equipment coupled with extreme lightness of weight will suffice, and a trip to a specialist shop selling such gear should be undertaken. At the same time it will be possible to inspect and discuss all the ancillary equipment, too.

For family use it will depend on how you spend your holidays, as well as the number of people normally in your party. Couples who tend to tour on a one-night stand basis want a small tent which can be erected and dismantled in a short amount of time, so either a two-man ridge tent or a small frame tent will be suitable. On the other hand, a larger party will require quite a big tent which, together with all the other gear, will occupy a lot more room in the car.

In consequence many people find it necessary to add a baggage trailer to carry their load, thus freeing the car interior of all extraneous items and making the journey less arduous.

What to look for when buying depends on the type of tent you have in mind. Small nylon tents usually have lightweight aluminium poles with stub plates under them where they go onto the groundsheet. Check their overall weight and ease of assembly—plus how small they become when separated. Always look carefully at the points at which strain is likely to occur and satisfy yourself that they are adequately reinforced. Make sure that you have a 'rip-stop' material, evident by a superimposed 'fishnet' pattern weave of heavier gauge, and examine the quality and suppleness of the groundsheet material, which should not be prone to puncturing or easy cracking. Decide on the material make-up: cotton/cotton, nylon/nylon, cotton/nylon combinations. Establish that spares and service are readily available.

On cotton tents especially, pay attention to any area which comes directly into contact with any of the poles or frame. They should always have an extra strip of material stitched in to avoid water coming through due to the 'priming action' of the movement of the fabric against the poles or frame. Check that zips are of sturdy calibre and preferably in nylon, which is self-lubricating and less likely to seize up on you.

# The trailer tent

Another form of tent accommodation which has grown considerably in popularity over the last few years is the trailer tent which, in its basic form, is a frame tent fitted onto a trailer. By ingenious design, the tent can be erected in only a few minutes and has the advantage (to some people at least) that the sleeping compartment is off the ground (see Fig. 6).

Trailer tents come in two basic designs. One is quite small on the road, yet manages to expand to much larger proportions once on site—but which

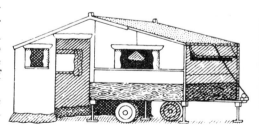

*Fig. 6 Trailer tent on site*

requires as much pegging out as a conventional frame tent, despite the quicker and simpler erection procedure. The other type comes mainly from America or Canada and on the road is almost as big as a caravan in terms of the area taken up. Where it differs is in height. Instead of the full height of a caravan it reaches only to worktop height, so that sinks, cookers and so on are ready for use.

Then, once on site, the one-piece plastic lid can be raised, usually by cranking a handle, so that it rises in a horizontal plane to form the roof section. As it does so, it pulls with it the sidewalls which are in canvas. At each end there is usually a full-width shelf which pulls out and is supported by struts, angled to the bottom edge of the trailer body. These two shelves form a double bedroom at each end. Unless an annexe is added, no pegging out at all is required for this type of arrangement. On a few luxury models, the lid section is sometimes motorised and can be operated at the touch of a button. Erection is therefore swift and convenient.

# Setting up a tent

Different tents need different techniques to erect them. Whenever possible the bedding section should be kept dry, which means the outer section has to go up first. If the frame is external, then that section should be assembled first and the tent hung from it.

In opening a two-pole ridge tent make a careful note of the manner in which it was packed so that you can repack it the same way. Insert the pole spike carefully in the ridge hole and lay the back of the tent out with the rear pole in position. Fasten the door, and peg out the corners in an exact rectangle. Use lightweight metal pegs, pushing them in by hand. Erect the rear pole, and peg headline (guy). Erect front pole and peg headline. Peg the corner guys, taking them out in a straight line with the seams of the tent. Next peg the middle guys, and the walls. (See Fig. 7.)

In the case of large frame tents, the roof section of the frame plus the first section of the legs should be erected, so that the tent is in a 'kneeling' position. Then throw the canvas section over the top, raise the legs two at a time and peg out, doing the corner sections first (see Fig. 8). Always be sure to close all zips beforehand, so that the corner points may be stretched laterally to hold the canvas firmly in place. The inner sections and any ancillary equipment can then be arranged at leisure, without anything getting wet if the weather happens to be inclement.

Pegs should normally be driven in at an angle approaching 45 degrees to the ground (see Fig. 9). This puts them into 'direct shear' with the guy ropes or rubber tensioners, which themselves leave the tent at a similar angle. Small skewer pegs may be used to secure the groundsheet corners of any inner section, or, with pup tents, to do the entire job. Double pegging or the use of larger versions may be necessary at strategic stress points, when strong winds are blowing.

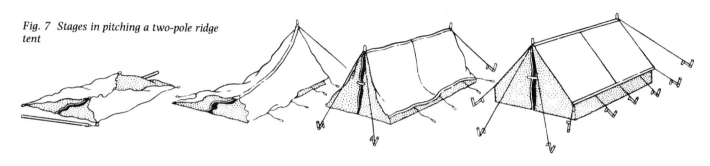

Fig. 7 Stages in pitching a two-pole ridge tent

Larger ridge tents are a little more trouble to erect, especially when there are few people about to lend a hand. In most cases, the technique is to first assemble the frame on the ground (except with 'A' frame models), then raise it into its working position. It takes two to hold the poles at this juncture, whilst two more people throw the canvas over them and peg out the vital holding points. These are the fore and aft guy ropes, followed by the four corners of the base unit. After that, it is all plain sailing.

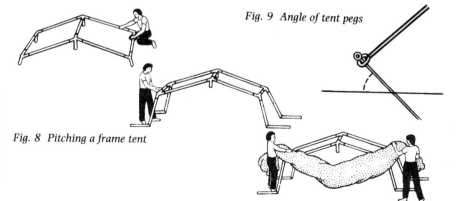

Fig. 9 Angle of tent pegs

Fig. 8 Pitching a frame tent

11

# Equipment

## Beds and bedding

Campbeds do still exist and some people prefer to be just those few inches off the ground as a result of using them. It is now far more common, however, to opt for the inflatable air bed, as this provides the heat insulation necessary to maintain body temperature. With raised frame campbeds, it is somewhat doubtful if this is so when a possible current of cold air is given free passage underneath. However, if space is not a serious problem, a combination of the two could be considered. But the use today of a campbed in this country is of doubtful advantage.

Airbeds come in two types—the better known inflatable type with its ribbed sections to 'hold us in' when asleep (see Fig.10), and the more recent pattern, shaped rather like a conventional domestic box mattress. Both do an identical job. The newer pattern is perhaps more comfortable. Backpackers must be more spartan, and usually opt for foam plastic mats which give them insulation at least, if not much comfort. They will wrap up into extremely lightweight rolls which can be enclosed in polythene bags and strapped under the packs.

## The importance of warmth

When sleeping on or near the ground, it is very important to maintain body temperature, or serious consequences could result from hyperthermia, in which death can occur in extreme cases. In an emergency situation even sheets of newspaper can be used to insulate the body from the ground. Keeping one's feet warm seems to be one of the criteria in terms of comfort, and bedsocks can be used to assist in this.

Winter backpacking is even more critical, as is any type of camping carried out above the snow line, even in the height of summer. Special equipment is needed and it is normal to sleep fully dressed—even with one's boots on under certain circumstances.

## The sleeping bag

Today, the almost universal form of bedclothing is the sleeping bag. It makes good sense since even with the pinning of blankets cold air could still permeate to the sleeper. Sleeping bags vary in quality—and accordingly, in price too. For simple summer camping under good weather conditions, an economical model costing between £10 and £20 should suffice. It will probably be filled with terylene wool and will be made in nylon fabric.

Better quality models, costing about £50 each, use specialist man-made fibres such as 'Hollofil'. This is based on the hair structure of the Canadian moose, each hair being hollow, to retain air and so give improved insulation. Man has now learned to simulate this with terylene type plastics and the results even approach the best filler of all—pure goose down. This latter type of filling is now extremely expensive and a good bag with this filling may cost upward of £150. They are therefore the province of the experienced and hardened mountaineer.

There are, of course, pros and cons for each type. The man-made bags will not rot and can be more readily laundered. Down, on the other hand, is very fragile in this respect and it needs a large degree of skill to handle it properly and avoid 'clumping' of the filling.

Bags come in two basic shapes. There is the rectangular shape which is good for normal camping under favourable conditions (see Fig. 11). It has the advantage that it can be zipped together with another of the same size to form a double sleeping bag. It will also serve as additional bedclothing around the house when not in use (an excellent way to keep it aired during the winter months).

Up-market bags, used for more severe conditions, are usually 'mummy' shaped, with a tapered effect towards the feet and a complete hooded shroud to keep out any cold air. For make no mistake about it, you can get cold more easily by air coming in at the top than by air permeating the sleeping bag insulation. There can be a drawstring on any type of sleeping bag which enables you to pull the bag tightly around your neck in cold weather—the 'mummy' type leaves only your nose out for breathing.

## Buying a bag

Choice is considerable and the best approach is to think about the use to which it will be put. A cheap one is sufficient for the annual holiday in Spain, but not for a winter weekend in Scotland. Whilst it is important to buy one sufficient to your needs, 'over buying' in terms of price will produce a bag which will be too hot and give you just as bad a night as one which is barely warm enough.

The construction, as well as the filling, is important. A good bag will have stitched separations between the sections in its design. This prevents the shifting around of the filling, which would destroy the even insulation of the sleeping bag.

A further good design aspect to watch for, especially on the more expensive bags, is whether the front zip is

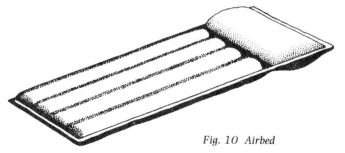

Fig. 10  Airbed

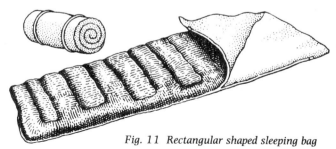

Fig. 11  Rectangular shaped sleeping bag

13

adequately guarded by a protective strip running throughout its length. The purpose of this is to prevent cold air entering at this point. The general condition and quality of the stitching is important too, especially in relation to a certain amount of reinforcement where major stresses occur.

Another important consideration when choosing a bag is the size and weight, especially if you are backpacking. Down is far the lightest in weight and will compress to a remarkably small size for packing. It will, however, quickly 'loft' to its original shape when taken out of its carrying sack.

Hollofil bags usually weigh twice as much as down bags and take about twice the amount of space. However, price-wise, they are only about a third of the cost to buy—yet afford as much as 90% of the efficiency of the down bag. They also wash much more easily—although this operation can be avoided as often as possible by using cotton liners, which are readily laundered at the end of each major trip.

The run of the mill bags are normally filled with a terylene wool or similar man-made fibre and come in two basic sizes—standard and 'king size' for the larger person. They are designated by weight, too, at 38 oz and 44 oz. However it should be realised that a king sized bag at 44 oz is scarcely any warmer than a standard 38 oz bag, since the available insulation in the former is spread around a larger area.

## Hints and tips on bedding

There is a certain art in preparing the bedroom for maximum comfort. The airbed, for example, should never be inflated too hard. The normally accepted test for the correct amount of air is to sit on it, when the base of the spine should just about touch bottom. Then, when you are lying flat, the additional area covered will leave you always with air underneath, yet shape the contours of the bed to your body for maximum support and comfort.

The bags are inevitably going to be affected by body warmth and perspiration and need to be aired inside-out for a few minutes each day, even if you are setting off for new horizons. (One of the factors affecting hypothermia is a loss of body temperature through moisture. This can just as easily be caused by internal moisture as by moisture which comes from the elements.) So ensure always that your equipment is kept as dry as possible.

# Camping furniture

For the lightweight camper, furniture becomes almost non-existent, except perhaps for the most rudimentary and smallest of folding stools. Even then, it becomes more the province of the small car camper, rather than the backpacker or the cycle camper. So to all intents and purposes, the furniture described will apply to the 'frame tenters' or 'trailer tenters'. For them, the sky is the limit so long as their cars or baggage trailers will take it in terms of space and payload. So tables, chairs, chaises-longues, cooking stands and so on are all permitted as part and parcel of the equipment.

Furniture can be made of two main materials and is normally in tubular form. Steel is heavier than aluminium but is, in general terms, stronger. It can, however, rust if not looked after. So, decisions have to be made as to whether lightness in weight or sheer strength is the most important factor. In all cases, since a table and four chairs are reasonably bulky, pay particular attention to how everything folds down when not in use, as this can make a big difference when packing (see Fig. 12).

The seating itself is usually in canvas, either cotton or man-made. The latter is probably the best, as it does not absorb water if it happens to get left out in the rain when you are off camp. Some more luxurious seats and chaises-longues are foam padded for extra comfort. Fine, but do bear in mind the extra amount of bulk when choosing. Cooking stands come in several forms, but by far the most popular is the 'Beanstalk' kitchen, which folds almost to nothing, yet gives a normal worktop height for the cooker (see Fig. 13). It has windshields to prevent flame blowout and provides at least one extra midway shelf for the utensils. 'Extras' are available to provide even more storage space.

# Lighting

Lighting in your tent can be provided for in a number of ways. You can use a small gas lamp or you can connect a lamp into the battery of your car, using either a tungsten filament or a fluorescent tube. These latter units are also available in portable versions, using dry cell batteries.

For the backpacker, two choices are available—the miniature gas lamp which uses a throw away cartridge

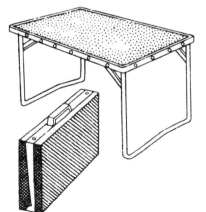

*Fig. 12  Folding table*

*Fig. 13  The 'Beanstalk' kitchen*

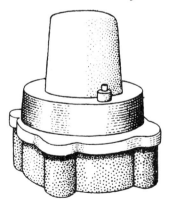

*Fig. 14  Portable battery lamp*

and a portable torch-like lamp which uses batteries (see Fig. 14). Of the two, the battery version is far safer, as the gas lamp, used inadvertently, could easily start a fire. However, this type of lamp is still useful due to the large amount of light given off, is economical to run and can double-up for use outside the tent when eating or relaxing as a group (see Fig. 15).

Frame tenters or trailer tenters have a lot more choice of appliances and, because they come by vehicle, are able to use bigger, more powerful lamps. Gas lamps for them can be fitted to the largest of the Camping Gaz cylinders (the 907) so that they have a solid base and are unlikely to tip over. By using an intermediate suspension hook, they may even be hung onto one of the roof struts.

When it comes to electric lighting, the majority opt for the modern fluorescent tube lighting which can be run on 12 volts DC by means of transistorised circuitry. This makes them infinitely safer to use than the mains versions sometimes fitted to caravans. However, it should be stressed that the tubes themselves are still rated for 240

volt running and so the units should *always* be disconnected before any examination or dismantling.

Two power sources are favoured: using either an auxiliary battery in the tent, or the one in the car. The alternative is to use a purpose-built transformer unit which gives a suitable 12 volt DC outlet. In either case, the battery or unit should have suitable plug and socket connectors, as crocodile clips could spark if knocked off and ignite the gases given off by a battery. An appropriate length of cable should therefore be fitted permanently to the lamp unit. (Special units are available which have clips for easy attachment to a roof strut of the tent.)

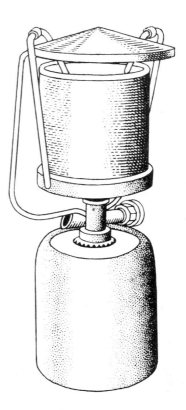

*Fig. 15  Portable gas lamp*

# Cooking

## The cooking stove

Camp cooking will depend on the sort of camping under consideration. For the backpacker ultimate weight is a vital factor, as too is the ability of the stove to function in windy weather or at high altitudes. Two basic types are available: the type which uses a loose liquid such as paraffin or even petrol and that using LPG (liquid petroleum gas). The former is favoured by mountaineers as it tends to be more efficient and a lot more economical to run. It also has a fiercer flame which is far more resistant to the effects of wind. Because it is pressurised, it is not affected, either, by thinner air at the higher altitudes (see Fig. 16).

Far more popular, however, among nearly all other campers, even of the lightweight category, is the miniature butane stove (see Fig. 17). This usually comes with expendable cartridges which last about two hours each. For the backpacker, there is a half size cartridge pattern which contains a small percentage of propane in the contents for added efficiency in cold weather.

Frame tent campers use a much larger refillable cylinder, since they are not weight conscious to the odd few pounds. This type can be bought in either butane or propane, according to requirements. There are two basic differences between propane and butane. They not only require different regu-

lators because they operate at different pressures, but also 'boil' at different temperatures (at which point they begin to change from liquid into gas). Butane ceases to do so effectively at about 3 degrees centigrade and so will not be efficient or even gas at all if cold weather is encountered. Propane, on the other hand, will continue to gas to as low as $-43$ degrees centigrade and is therefore essential for cold weather use. This is why the small cartridges sometimes used by mountaineers and backpackers actually contain a mixture.

Regulators are not interchangeable and in Europe neither are the Calor Gas cylinders refillable (for those who use

 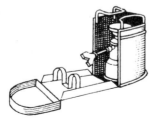  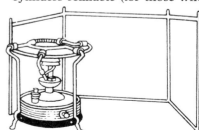

*Fig. 16  Portable stoves*

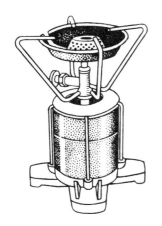

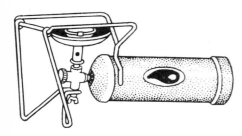

*Fig. 17  Portable gas stoves*

the bigger quantities). Camping Gaz, in all its forms, is well distributed, but its larger sized cylinders are available only in butane gas.

Stoves used by frame tent and trailer tent campers are normally of double-burner type, usually with a grill as well (see Fig. 18). Use of a cooking stand therefore becomes more or less necessary if comfort is to be considered. The stove is usually fed by one of the larger cylinders mentioned earlier, which provides a fairly long duration of use and therefore gives scope for more varied cooking. Most are geared to run on butane, but will normally operate almost as well on propane (to U.K. standards at 14" water gauge pressure). In other words, only the cylinder regulator needs to be changed. Burner jets can cope with the propane up to this pressure without modification.

*Fig. 18  Double burner stove*

## Barbecue units

The barbecue has gained in popularity over the last few years and is now favoured by many campers (see Fig. 19). However, although it is a very pleasant method of cooking some dishes (straight over glowing embers), it does involve a fair amount of work and attention and is more for the camper who wants to relax, than for the one who is out and about most of the time. It does lend itself especially to family groups using the larger equipment, where space on site and in transit is quite adequate.

Barbecues *do make smoke*, however they are organised and this, unfortunately, is not always acceptable on campsites.

There are similar devices, loosely termed 'barbecues', which run on butane or propane gas and are in reality gas grills. They work well and will swiftly dispatch a quantity of sausages, steaks, chops, etc, with a pleasant grilled finish. They do *not*, however, impart that smoky barbecue flavour. They do not smoke, but cook from overhead or from the side, so that any fat running off drips into a tray and not

18

*Fig. 19 Small portable barbecue*

onto the embers. As a result, they are not so unpopular among other campers as are the conventional barbecues.

## Bonfires

Bonfires should *never* be lit on *any* campsite or private land without the prior permission of the owner or management.

In certain areas in continental Europe, especially where there is abundant forestry and a hot climate to go with it, bonfires and even barbecues are strictly forbidden. Notices to that effect are displayed quite clearly, usually by a pictorial representation of a small fire with a diagonal red line struck through it.

Other safety factors should always be taken into account when handling fire in any shape or form. LPG cylinders, for example, are perfectly safe to use if the normal precautions are taken and the manufacturer's instructions followed to the letter. *Never, never* change a cylinder (and still less a cartridge which has no shut-off valve) in the vicinity of, or upwind from, another appliance which is alight. Propane, for instance, expands to 250 times its volume when released from the cylinder. Not only is it inflammable, but a mere 2% dilution with air is an explosive mixture and should be respected as such.

When changing large cylinders, *always* first shut off the valve and make sure that all throw-away cartridges are completely empty before undoing the base of the stove and releasing them.

## Cooking utensils

These will, of course, vary to some extent according to the type of camping you decide to do (see Fig. 20). For lightweight and backpacking campers, there are many specialised bits and pieces so small it is difficult to believe they exist. Some very small stoves, weighing no more than about a pound, are encased in tiny spun aluminium containers which double as saucepans.

On the other hand, the larger tent camper needs more scope as family needs have to be catered for. Ideally, a nest of pots is probably the best choice. They are readily available from nearly every camping store and consist of three to four saucepans, one inside the other, with the lid doubling up as a frying-pan. In latter years, these are generally teflon-coated and therefore non-stick in character. This in turn helps along that awkward chore, the washing up. The nest will probably have a couple of detachable handles for lifting the saucepans on and off the stove, plus their individual lids. Whilst the lids are adequate as frying-pans, they are not very big, and it is probably safer to use a standard domestic version with a fixed handle, despite the slightly additional bulk involved when packing the gear.

## Water containers

These are many and varied, from straight 'jerrycan' types in plastic, to more sophisticated 'garden roller' versions which are favoured by many people. The reason for their popularity is that it is very easy to transport quite large quantities of water at one time and thereby reduce the job to one which even the children can manage without help. For the lightweight camper there are flexible plastic containers which fold down to almost nothing when empty. Some will hang from the tent pole and are fitted with a tap. There are even a few obtainable made from a black plastic material, so the hanging 'bottle' forms a solar heating device and warms the contents in a surprisingly short space of time.

## Crockery and cutlery

As with saucepans, the manufacturers have done a fairly good job in providing specialist items. There are crockery sets (in plastic materials of course) and sets

Fig. 20  A selection of cooking items

20

of cutlery, sometimes as individual sets in their own little pochettes. Then there are items such as a tin-opener, bottle opener and maybe even a cork-screw—all of which can be bought at the local hardware store.

## Food storage

One vital point to remember is that food should not be stored at ground level, where it can be attacked by insects and small animals. There are special hanging larders, zipped and ventilated, to cope with the situation. There are ice boxes too for those who camp in the grander style—or even small refrigerators which will run off gas or mains electricity on site and on 12 volts DC from the car whilst en route.

Items such as tea, sugar, coffee, etc can be stored in screwtop jars (like those in which you buy most instant coffee). Pepper and salt are usually bought in sealed containers anyway. Tinned food presents no problem. For the lightweight camper, who is really concerned with every ounce of weight, there are special dehydrated foods obtainable from many specialist camping shops around the country.

# Clothing

The underlying theme of camping is 'freedom', so the last thing you want to do is dress up in clothing which is not comfortable. However, there are many other considerations which bear an important influence on exactly what 'comfort' is in specific terms.

Two prime factors have to be considered: clothing which keeps you dry and clothing which keeps you warm—both being very closely interconnected and dependent on each other. Basic casual clothing is the right approach: slacks or jeans, pullovers and anoraks seem to be appropriate for ordinary family camping, together with lightweight waterproofs in the form of leggings and lightweight anoraks (see Fig. 21).

With this theme as a base on which to work out your wardrobe, you can ring the changes as many times as you want, according to the weather. Several pullovers will enable differences in temperature to be taken care of. The waterproof lightweight anorak will take care of the rain and the heavier version of colder weather.

If it is also a heavy waterproof model, so much the better. Lightweight leggings will protect your legs from prolonged rain. All these items of clothing will throw together in a rucksack or a holdall bag. None will be any the worse for being somewhat screwed up.

Footwear may vary from heavy shoes, to heavier boots if much walking is contemplated, to 'wellies' if the weather turns sour and leaves you in wet grass or mud. For winter camping and mountaineering work, specialist anoraks and other equipment is available. Anoraks can be in down-filled nylon or Hollofil—or may be in terylene filling similar to that used in the more basic sleeping bags. Overgear in lightweight, siliconised nylon fabrics has to be of stouter stuff to avoid tearing or damage by high winds. Boots must be fitted with more advanced soles and crampons may even be carried or worn if the snowline is encountered.

Socks should be of thick wool, with possibly a lighter pair—also wool—inside. Avoid nylon as it causes perspiration and blistering. Socks should be washed and changed as often as possible and always dried before wearing. Boots should always be kept in good condition which means they should be both supple and waterproof. This is best achieved by treating them frequently to a thorough soaking (not immersion) in liquid dubbin, mars oil or neatsfoot oil, which can be brushed in. Always carry a spare set of laces.

In cold weather, gloves or mittens may be needed and these should, if possible, be of a waterproof material. Ski shops can sometimes come up with something suitable for the job. Headgear may be varied from a simple sou'wester for rain, to a 'bobble hat' in wool for colder weather. Balaclava type designs are good here, as they provide better coverage of the face.

In summer time at a reasonable altitude, ordinary holiday clothing will suffice, although raingear is always a wise precaution in the United Kingdom. Clothing can be hung from a special fitting on an *upright* pole in the tent structure (that is, on the larger tents). Cover with a plastic bag (inverted) to inhibit dampness in wet weather. In pup tents you have no room to hang clothing and, unless you have a car, spare items have to be packed away when not in use.

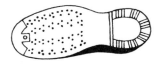

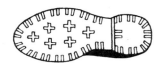

*Fig. 21 Clothing and footwear for camping*

22

# Hygiene and sanitation

These are two vital matters which can alienate people from campers more quickly than anything else if the proper steps are not taken. On sites, there is seldom any problem with either aspect, since facilities are provided and it is easy to maintain both personal and general hygiene. When camping 'wild', however, it is an entirely different matter. Then, proper precautions must be taken to dig the appropriate latreens (even on a once only basis).

Where streams are used for solo style lightweight camping, check that there is no up-stream pollution and that you do not offend others by your behaviour. Waste water should be disposed of by tipping it into a small hole or pit dug for the purpose and not thrown away irresponsibly into the hedgerows unless it is first filtered to remove grease and scum.

For family campers, portable toilet units are becoming increasingly popular. Many families use them even where full facilities exist in order to avoid a sometimes lengthy trip during the night or in bad weather.

They come in two basic types: one in which you have what is little more than a plastic bucket and seat arrangement (possibly with a separate liner). The second and more widely-used sort has two distinct compartments: the bowl section, usually fitted with its own handpumped flush, and a base section in which the waste is not only stored, but is rendered inoffensive by the use of special formaldehyde-based chemicals. The bottom section is normally shut off by a hand- or foot-operated sluice valve. The larger version allows the base to be detached for easy disposal, whereas the smaller one is normally built as an integral unit.

Some tents have a small built-in annexe into which the toilet unit can be placed, for direct access from inside; but in most cases, the use of a small toilet tent seems to be preferred (see Fig. 22). This arrangement is favoured by many ardent rally enthusiasts, since it gives an increased degree of privacy when entertaining guests on site.

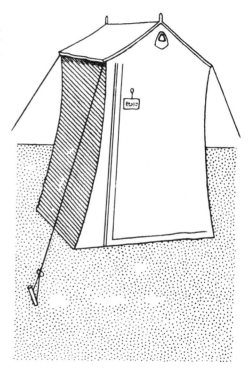

*Fig. 22 Lightweight toilet tent*

23

# First aid outfits

Everyone has his or her own idea of what should be carried, but the standard commercially available kit usually contains most of the necessary ingredients. For some bandages substitute, perhaps, a few more plasters, elastic bandages and, if walking, a couple of crepe bandages to cope with sprains and the like. To this, you can add such items as Alka-Seltzer, paracetamol, laxatives, pills for 'Continental tummy' or similar intestinal problems, as well as insect repellants and antihistamines. The latter covers treatment for wasp and bee stings and mosquito bites. For snake bites you should seek medical attention. However, there are now a few devices which can be used with some success in the case of snake bites. One of these, the 'Aspi-Venim' from France, comprises a small plastic plunger device looking something like a hyperdermic syringe. It works by creating a partial vacuum over the bite and the poison is drawn out at source. The inventor claims that the danger from snake bites is largely eliminated.

# The rucksack

Extreme lightweight campers who go in for backpacking do, in fact, have to carry everything they possess on their backs, so it follows that the rucksack is an item of equipment about which no inconsequential decision should be taken. It becomes a vital link in the chain and can make all the difference between walking relatively comfortably or groaning at every step you take.

There are two basic types of rucksack available: a frame type, in which the sack itself is braced by a steel or aluminium frame, or the ergonomic type which is designed to fit snugly to the contours of your back. Both have their followers and both have different advantages and disadvantages. The frame type is slightly more rigid in its application, but will allow air to circulate around and over the back. The ergonomic type tends to keep the back over-warm and you may then risk a chill when finally you part company with it.

Shoulder straps should be well padded to avoid chafing and any leather fittings tanned with chromic salts to avoid rotting. The more modern ones, with a padded waist harness to draw the sack onto the hips, are probably more comfortable in the long run than those which do not have this facility. Otherwise they tend to drag on the shoulders and eventually become rather uncomfortable. With a bit of careful planning the all-up weight should be feasible at a mere 25 lbs or so. Beyond that, the pack becomes tedious.

Of course, some stalwarts carry much heavier loads – it depends on the size and strength of the backpackers. The above figure is only an average guide. It will depend also on the space taken up by, and the weight of, items such as sleeping bags. The difference between a pure duvet bag and one in, say, Hollofil is quite considerable.

The rucksack should be packed so that any sharp or hard objects do not end up in a position where they might be uncomfortable against the back of the wearer. A correct sequence, too, is important so that items required during the day are packed near the top. If not, the entire rucksack may have to be disturbed unnecessarily. (See Fig. 23.)

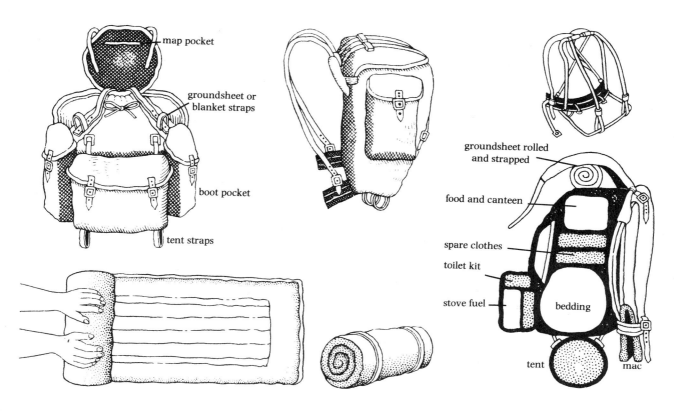

map pocket

groundsheet or
blanket straps

boot pocket

tent straps

groundsheet rolled
and strapped

food and canteen

spare clothes

toilet kit

stove fuel

bedding

tent

mac

Fig. 23 Packing the rucksack

# Specific forms of camping

## Camping in mountains

This form of camping needs very specialised equipment. Mountains must at all times be considered as potentially dangerous terrain, even if the actual gradient is negotiable on foot without any elaborate climbing tackle. Weather is probably the biggest enemy and must be guarded against at all times. *Always* carry warm items of clothing, emergency rations, a torch, a first aid kit, a whistle, good large-scale maps and a compass, in addition to your normal camping items. Yet the total weight you carry should, if anything, be even lighter than for ordinary camping. At high altitudes oxygen is reduced, and this can make the going very tough at times.

There are special tents (see Fig. 24), special sleeping bags, food, stoves, etc, as well as high quality heat insulation and waterproofed garments to wear. Always go prepared for the worst possible weather conditions and *never*

Fig. 24

alone. Three seems to be the agreed optimum number in a small party, as this number is more able to cope in an emergency.

Pitch in the leeway of the wind if you camp aloft, as this is the most likely factor to induce hypothermia—loss of body temperature. Dampness is the second big factor. Wet clothing should be avoided by adding lightweight nylon over garments. Avoid, too, the dampness caused by excessive perspiration from inside. It can be just as conducive to hypothermia as rain from the outside. It is best avoided by wearing apparel which will 'breathe'. Wool is ideal but is not waterproof. Completely impermeable garments won't 'breathe' and so compromise has to be reached. In recent years, manufacturers have developed fabrics (Gortex) with 95% waterproof properties yet which allow the body to breathe.

Several layers of lightweight clothing are always superior to having a single heavier garment and are also far more comfortable to wear. Speciality mountaineering in which either climbing or potholing is involved needs extra care. Snow conditions may have to be taken into account and, underground, flood water can be a real hazard in bad weather conditions. Finally, always take stock of weather conditions before setting out and *always* let somebody know your route and destination, plus your expected estimated time of arrival (ETA) back to base. In that way, rescue squads will know where to look for you should you inadvertently run into trouble.

# Cycle camping

Cycle camping is another form of lightweight activity, but with more scope in terms of what you can carry and how far you can go. Much of the smaller type of gear is applicable for this sort of camping. It is in the method of carrying it that this mode differs most. Forget your rucksack and any means of carrying a load at a high level, such as on your back. Keep the centre of gravity low by investing in specialised carriers which are fitted to the bike itself (see Fig. 25). In that way, life will be rendered more comfortable.

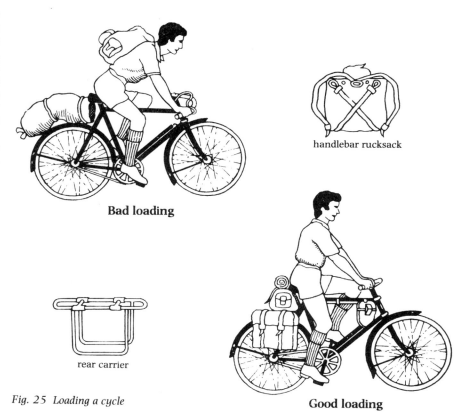

handlebar rucksack

**Bad loading**

rear carrier

*Fig. 25 Loading a cycle*

**Good loading**

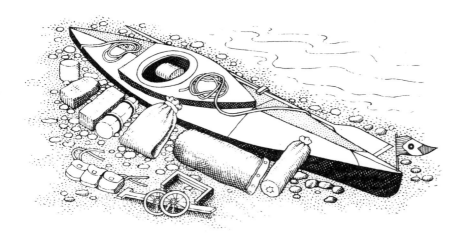

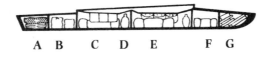

A B C D E F G

A Spare clothes B Stove, etc. C Bedding
D Water E Food and odd items in hold-alls
F Tent G Carriage repair outfit

*Fig. 26 Storing equipment in a 2-man canoe*

Motor cycle camping is similar in many ways to cycle camping; the possibilities for load distribution are greater but there may be two passengers rather than one. Once again, carriers placed against the rear wheel areas and securely fastened to the frame are favoured. Because weight is kept lower than on a bike, a small, lightweight load may be added to a special tank rack on the front.

## Canoe camping

Canoe camping has its own specialist safety applications. Water is always potentially dangerous and should never be taken for granted. There are other inherent problems too. All the gear, if carried on the canoe itself, as when touring, must be suitably housed in plastic bags to keep it bone dry, whatever happens (see Fig. 26). When pitching overnight, avoid low-lying banks which might be prone to flooding.

## Boat camping

This comes into two categories. One is similar to canoe camping, in which

*Fig. 27 Punt with canopy*

you stop nightly at a convenient spot and pitch your tent. The second category is when you use a suitable craft like a punt in which to actually sleep, pulling a top canopy across the boat for protection against the elements (see Fig. 27). Remember, if you are taking a separate tent, that mooring or pitching tents on private riverside land is not allowed.

If camping in the boat itself, make allowances for possible tidal effects which can leave a small craft at an alarming angle during the night if it touches bottom on a steep sided bank. Rivers where tides come and go rapidly can also be dangerous, since incoming tides react almost like floodwater and can overturn a small boat.

# Family camping

There is no doubt that children enjoy camping as much as, or even more than, adults. Little attention is necessary for children over the age of eight in family camps, although an early bedtime is desirable if full benefits are to be gained.

It is the young child from six months upwards that may raise doubts in the minds of parents as to the wisdom of camping. They can rest assured that almost from the Camping and Caravanning Club's inception young babies have been taken to camp, using little more than the equipment shown in these pages. These babies have now brought their children and their children's children into the camping fraternity. These notes are for the parents who are new to camping ways.

With the young baby there need be no fears in summer on account of the weather if a sound tent and flysheet are used on a protected site; avoid exposed or crowded sites. Baby can sleep in a carry-cot on a level with the mother's bed. Night feeding or other attention can be given by the light of an electric torch and a small spirit stove used for heating liquids. Small canvas baths are easily available.

The toddler will sleep best in a large folding pram that he is already used to. The child should ideally have a sleeping compartment separate from the parents.

Serve children's meals at the times they are used to at home. Protect the child's head during the middle part of the day from direct sun with a sun hat (older children can wear a scarf, gypsy fashion) and cover the shoulders with a loosely worn 'cowboy scarf'.

Protect children's ears, fingers and bare legs in cold, windy weather. Woollen ankle socks should be worn for walking to avoid blisters.

Children should be allowed their favourite toys. A book or two, crayons, plain paper in book form will fill in the time on a rainy day.

The journey to and from the campsite can sometimes be a problem when children are at a certain age. Try sorting out a few special games for them to play whilst in the car, such as spotting certain makes of car or collecting number plates.

# Good camping

## Country manners

Most country people look upon visitors as guests. Therefore shed your townsman's reserve and be ready to speak and act in an open and hospitable manner to people you meet. To avoid offending farmers, observe the following simple rules:

**Gates.** If a gate is shut when you come to it, leave it shut when you have passed through. Sometimes a farmer leaves the gate open on purpose so that cattle can pass through unattended, so if you come to a wide open gate, do not shut it behind you. Do not climb over closed gates, always use the latch.

**Grassland.** You will not damage grazing grass by walking across it, but mowing grass (which can be distinguished by its length and general appearance of being undisturbed by cattle should not be walked on.

**Crops.** Never walk across a field growing crops; if you have permission to cross such ground walk on the grass verge round the edge of the field.

**Hedges and fences.** It is a crime to make a hole in a fence. Once a hole is made a farmer may have continual trouble from cattle trying to push through. Avoid climbing over fences to make short cuts; there will be at least one gate or stile in every field.

**Cattle.** It is preferable to insist as a condition of paying fees for a field site that cattle are not grazed while campers are in occupation. Never allow children to chase cattle. Do not empty water into animal feeding troughs.

**Farm machinery.** Remember that a farmer's implements are the tools of his trade. Prevent children from playing on machines, it can be damaging to life and limb, and also to the machinery.

**Do not leave litter** round the site, along the road, or in villages. Do not shout, sing or make a noise ('revving' car) after 10 p.m. or before 7 a.m.

## General hints

Have consideration for other campers. Approach sites directly and openly from the front.

If you are in charge of young people, ban 'tent raiding' and other thoughtless games.

In wet weather be careful not to touch the sides of the tent, as this will draw rain through the fabric. Keep all bedding rolled in groundsheets, away from sides of tent.

Put kit on top of bedding.

In a high wind, lock guys on runner slots and double peg. Flysheets or roofs should be storm set. The crossed lines are to stop billowing; they should not touch the tent. Headlines should be pegged out in front of doors. Never leave canvas unattended for longer than is necessary. Never light a fire inside a tent. If a tent has to be packed wet it should be unpacked within 12 hours and dried away from heat.

Scrape pegs clean, and pack in a separate bag.

Mud splashes can be cleaned from canvas with soap and warm water. Reproofing the tent occasionally will keep the fabric in good condition and maintain its rain-shedding properties. Granger-sol 'Canvaclean' both cleans and reproofs.

# Choosing a camp site

There are a large number of Camping and Caravanning Club sites throughout the country. Club members receive a sites list which gives a brief description of the sites, together with details such as water supply, shops, etc. Also most of the large suppliers of camp gear stock commercial site books for both Britain and the Continent. The motoring organisations supply their members with similar information.

If you are in a locality where no sites are listed enquire at the local Post Office, police, R.A.C. or A.A. You should then have a choice of site to suit your needs.

Those who seek privacy may wish to approach land-owners on their own initiative. Remember, farmers are busy people, a respectful approach is the first requirement without a previous introduction. *Never camp without asking permission* even on so-called 'common land', which means 'common grazing land'—not 'common ownership'. Look for the following points:

**Choose a spot** affording shelter from the prevailing winds, on a well-drained, fairly level soil and facing the morning sun—if possible select a site with a pleasant and interesting view. A field corner with a hedge that offers protection from the wind is quite suitable, whilst the fringe of a wood or the lower side of a clump of trees if camping on a hill are also good sites.

The site should not be too far from drinking water. If the camp is to be for more than a few days, it should not be too far from supplies. Whatever spot is selected try to have a pleasant view from the tent door. Let it be an open one; glades among trees become dull and uninteresting, and tend to give one a sense of confinement, particularly if it becomes necessary to spend a long period in the tent owing to bad weather.

# Camping hints

Slacken guys slightly at night and in wet weather (unless they are fitted with rubber tensioners). Tighten them in the morning when the dew or rain has dried out. Over-slackness may result in the tent blowing down in high wind. In soft ground or exposed positions corner guys should have extra pegs and lines.

Air ground daily, if possible. Bedding can be laid out on a groundsheet, or hung up to air. Tent walls and even roofs of lightweight tents can be thrown back to let maximum sun and air reach the ground.

**Make sure of:**
Adequate and good water supply. Remember average requirements are two gallons per head per day—one gallon for washing, half a gallon for cooking and half a gallon for drinking.

A fairly private site that will not be overlooked or encourage trespassers. Be sure to obtain permission first before pitching camp.

Reasonable access to public transport and quite near supplies.

**Avoid:**

Deep woods where the sun cannot penetrate. Do not pitch immediately under a tree—the raindrops drip a long time after the rain has stopped! Avoid elm or beech trees from which branches often fall.

Long or rank grass should be avoided—it is often wet in dry weather and harbours midges and other unpleasant insects.

Low lying or marshy land and bare and exposed hilltops.

Clay soil as it is always cold and damp.

Land which may be prone to flooding from a nearby river – or even a lake – particularly if there has been an unusual amount of rain. Tidal rivers in particular can change their levels very suddenly.

Fields which show signs of being infested with ants or similar pests. They can make life very uncomfortable and are a nuisance where foodstuffs are concerned. Fields used by cattle, even if empty at the time can be messy to say the least, especially if you arrive at dusk, when it is not too easy to see the ground.

# The Camping and Caravanning Club

The Camping and Caravanning Club has its origin in the Association of Cycle Campers, founded in 1901 by T. H. Holding who initiated a revolution in camping. These pioneers made it possible for pedestrians and cyclists to carry their own kit. Years of experiment by Club members, freely giving time and money, have developed camping into what it is today, enjoyed by thousands all over the world.

Today the Club still carries on this forward outlook, new ideas are continually sought and tried out. The Club's officers are ready to help all who are willing to learn good camping.

The Club has fought restrictions which would have prevented camping over large areas of the country. One of the Club's aims is the establishment of adequate camping facilities in the National Parks.

The Club has secured for its members valuable exemptions with regard to camping under the Public Health Act, 1936, and The Town and Country Planning Act, 1971, but for the general good the Club has voluntarily imposed on its members certain restrictions.

The address of the Camping and Caravanning Club is:

11 LOWER GROSVENOR PLACE, LONDON, SW1W OEY.

Tel: 01 828 1012